Falling

Barney Norris

Published by Playdead Press 2012

© Barney Norris 2012

Barney Norris has asserted his rights under the Copyright, Design and Patents Act, 1988, to be identified as the author of this work.

A CIP catalogue record for this book is available from the British Library.

ISBN 978-0-9574491-2-1

Printed and bound in England by CMP (uk) Limited

This book is sold subject to the condition that it shall not by way of trade or otherwise, be lent, resold, hired out, or otherwise circulated without the publisher's prior consent in any form of binding or cover other than that in which it is published and without a similar condition including this condition being imposed on the subsequent purchaser.

Playdead Press
www.playdeadpress.com

By the same author:

Plays

At First Sight

Fear of Music

Acknowledgments are due to the editors of *Borderlines, The Fabelist, The Frogmore Papers, The Interpreter's House, The Literateur, The Owl, PITCH, The SHOp* and *The Westminster News,* where some of these poems first appeared.

The debts I have incurred in writing these are innumerable. Thank you.

For George.

Out of Office
7

To the Needles
8

Blowback
9

Fin Whale
10

Three Lives
12

The Wanderer
13

Histories
15

Falling
17

The Key
21

Overhearing
24

Good Night
25

To Music
26

Passing
27

Snow
28

The Cuckoo
30

The going down of the sun
32

The Solitary Reader
34

And by tracing it twice
35

Out of Office

Not in geography. There are satellites
to spot me, there are Streetviews
of places I've been. I'll hide here,
where no search can uncover
the speech of one line to another:
in the unGooglable world.

To the Needles

Here, the borderlands have the look
of distance, so you cut ahead,
and the cold in your fingers
fades away when you see the view,
where you stop in your tracks,
where the wind takes you full in the face.

They're down there, a row of stones
with the sea all about them, and birds
on their tips in the teeth of the wind.
And all you can hear is the wind, that sounds
like your own self parting the grass -
like your own self seen in a glass.

Blowback

Then for a little while there were days
of almost unbearable happiness.
They caught a bus to North Gorley and vanished
into a landscape buried in gorse
till she said she was hungry.
He took out Oranginas in their figlike bottles
and they sat with their legs crossed,
facing each other. She took from her purse
a packet of baccy, Rizla papers and a bag of hash,
and rolled, cupping her hands to her face
so he heard rather than saw the flame's flaring.
'Come here.' She filled her lungs
and put her mouth to his, opening his lips
with the tip of her tongue and breathing
in. They had sex for the first time
there on the bank among the rabbit sets.
He doubted he lasted a minute. But for as long
as his mouth was on her breasts,
as she pulled his jeans clear
of his heels, not speaking, not quite
stoned enough to lose all self-consciousness,
as long as he held the white
instep of her foot and her nails
scored him, touching, loving,
they felt as though they had invented something.

Fin Whale

He was always down the beach by four
to take out the boat. That night he hadn't slept
and gone down early, that was why
he got there first. The drizzle
was always that time of year, and he walked
with his collar up into the dark
of the hour before dawn coloured rain,
head down, knowing
there were no cars to watch for this hour.
But he always looked up to his lover, the water,
when the home road poured over the hill.
She lifted him almost out of himself.

That was when he saw it.
His spine blossomed up to the top.

What could he say of the view,
he liked to ask through foam
of a pint as he watched the bright eyes
of the listeners drinking him -
could you say it was big as a house?
A boat? Some ships, perhaps.
He stood speechless,
top of the hill, and knew
he was the only boy in the world
had ever seen this. He shared the light
with the creature for a minute,
then turned to wake the sleeping houses

from their murmuring retreats.
Afterwards, when the body was gone,
and the reporters and photographers
had come and gone,
their Dictaphones and USBs filled
like crab buckets with spoils of the strand line,
he started to doubt it had happened.
In the noise of that great wave
of flesh against the light, things had seemed
undeniable. But later,
in front of his two-bar and plunged
back into the dailyness of life,
it frightened him. After dark
he felt very small in the memory.
His was only an ordinary life, anyone
unused to the big world
would have been as shocked if it turned
to roar at them half as loud.

It had been like a great scream
in the face of everything he recognized
as sense. A vast affront.
When he lay down, he wondered why
the sea should want to shake him so hard
it felt the need to vomit
a monster up onto the mumbling shore.

Three Lives

A blackbird lands in a boy's hand, and
he freezes for it, quiet as a stone -

waiting for heat to stir in his palm.
Another puts a finger in a dam,

like Cuchulain, like Cnut, but winning.
The third has a worse time of it, hides

a fox in good will from a hunter,
loses his stomach, saying nothing.

Look closely. They are all the same boy.
They would have turned into the same man.

The Wanderer

From the Old English

Alone, we turn to working out
the world, although we know
there's little meaning in it –
we've spent time enough adrift
to work that out.
I heard one man tell it like this:
'Alone at dawn, I always turn
to working out the world.
There's no one living now
that I can talk to.
It's best to sit quiet
with thoughts like these.
Since she left I've bothered
no one. I cross the seas
instead, in search of a warm
pair of arms. Anyone
who's tried will tell you
what it's like, alone in a boat
with grief. You grow in
like a toenail and live
in the past, in a dream
of her body. When you wake
there's sea everywhere,
and shags and gulls and rain.
That doesn't help. You talk
to them but they don't

answer. You go on,
though you don't know why
or how. You know
you're getting older,
you're going to die.
That's called getting wiser.
It takes time and makes you
careful. You have visions
of the world after you've left it -
a grey-blue film-reel
for animals to stalk through,
a grandson burying everything
you ever made. The men
who get that far I've heard
tell it like this: Where
has everyone gone? God,
it's darker here, the place
is falling down under the rain.
Nothing lasts, does it.'
That's what I heard him say,
away from the world in thought.
I try to have some hope
myself. And I hope
it's best to sit quiet
apart and not talk,
and try to work out the world.

Histories

1.

It was her birthday, and she sank to her knees
when the call came to say he was dead.
Her youngest told his classmates *My grandad
didn't die in the war, he died in the car.*

Who knows what her mother thought:
did she reach over him, take the wheel,
and keep them on the road while his heart
gave out? Did she concentrate on steering?

Or did the life that passed in that moment
pass for a moment through her? Was the last sound
he heard the careful application
of breaks, or a voice, *Are you all right dear?*

2.

They are briefly together. He is on leave
from the Free French Navy. They
marry in the morning, and share a bottle
of sherry between themselves and their friends.

In the afternoon, one of the guests, who
drives a cab, gives them a ride to the station.
But two miles early he stops the car
and apologises - he's come to the end

of his petrol ration. They walk the rest
of the way. On the platform they kiss goodbye
and he leaves for the ports. It will be three years
before they see one another again.

Falling

She used to go to a dance
every Friday night.

There were nights in
halls all

over the city, and she
and her girlfriends

were young, and loved
to see

the different faces.
They would take hours

to dress
and do their hair,

then queue,
usually

in rain, to get in and
stand under the windows

of the hall, drink in hand,
watching the braver

dancers and the girls
who came with their partners.

How they hated them.

After nine, men
started asking,
and the group

would break up as one
by one the girls
were led onto the floor,

then sometimes
brought back to their place
at the edge

like they had been books
on loan, or otherwise
taken home afterwards.

Half the couples in town
at that time first met
on those evenings,

and she wouldn't have been
surprised if
half the children

of those years weren't
conceived in bedsits
and single beds a few hours

after a dance.

He wasn't a good mover
but he held her well,
and didn't do anything wrong,
and that was as much

as a girl could demand.
When he asked if she wanted
to go somewhere else
she was glad to follow him

out through the door
and the dark. He made them
coffee with whisky,
and they talked on the sofa

in his parent's front room.
She didn't speak
while she let him undress her.
He seemed scared

so she held his hand.
She told him she was a virgin,
and if he noticed otherwise
he never said.

And that was the start, or the end.

The Key

You called today
to say you'd seen
a new foal in the field

beyond the houses,
afterbirth still
on the ground.

I thought of the horses
that used to be trafficked
through our barn

when I was very young,
and of an afternoon
when I helped herd

a gang of calves
escaped from the next farm,
fearless, six.

I remembered
the Thunderbird stickers
I used to save for,

all gone now,
though I collected
all but one,

how we used to walk
to the shop in the village
for those

and penny sweets.
In our back field
buttercups grew

thick in summer,
and you held them
under my chin.

I liked butter.
One afternoon
the spare key fell

through a hole
in my boot while we played there
with the donkey,

and I remember
the rest of that afternoon
like the end of an episode,

us
picking through buttercups
looking for a key

I suppose must still
be out there, rusting,
as the day around us

fades to black
and my memory stops
before we get back

in the house.

Overhearing

Turn off all the lights in the house
and go into the garden. Perhaps
you can't see stars, some cities
are blind. But if there's a tree

you'll hear the song
of its leaves as they move in the wind.
Fix on that. Stand still. That sound
has been there all evening,

and will still speak after you sleep.
All the world is contained in the sound
of the things that continue without you –
the mystery of a leaf in the wind.

Good Night

From Muller

I was a stranger when I came here
and I'll leave like a stranger.
In May this place was beautiful –
the flowers, the weather, the girls

were beautiful. Now it's October
and everything's the colour of the road
ahead. We never get to choose
the season of our leaving.

I'll go by moonlight, following
the deer tracks, not looking back.
Love changes and loves changes,
so I'll wish you good night.

It wouldn't be fair to wake you.
Instead I'll slide a note under your door
to wish you good night.
And that's the last you'll hear

from me, *Good night
my love, good night.*
I'll walk all night to the beat of it.
Good night, my love, good night.

To Music

From von Schober

My love, in my grey hours,
when I am caught in the whorl of living,
you warm me into love
and out of myself.

Your self escaping as a sigh,
a quiet chord,
opens the heaven of the past
and lets us out.

Passing

There's no truth worth telling
that isn't a tree catching fire
at the bottom of the garden
at the beginning of autumn,

or the way the soil
backed up into the bank of a river
falls into the water under
a grey sky on a cold morning.

Snow

He longed to cram his mouth
with the light that flowered
in the sky that evening,
but it shocked his fingers
where he held, he didn't know
how it could be so white
to the touch.

What it covered and showed
in the square of garden,
all the blue bulbs hiding,
all the animals tracked
and revealed.

He loved to plummet down
on his uncle's sled, on the big
hill with the horses who ran
when he fell too fast,
when he shone like Icarus.

It tasted like Christmas.
Nights in or coming home,
feeling of family, feeling
of days in the heat of company,
overeating, venturing out
to crisp walks, heavy trees
bowing to hold him.

He read the road deaths.
He knew about murders
discovered much later, concealed
by the winter, people
found dead in their homes
and the radios going on
without them.

It didn't help him.
In his second year
at Birmingham he signed up
for the ski trip, travelled
to Val d'Isere,
drank more than he could bear,
lay down and was consumed
in the whiteness
of a snowdrift.

The Cuckoo

From Dafydd ap Gwilym

Voice on a grove branch,
clock in the wood,
latch of a loose shutter
ringing through the silence,
what distant place
are you back from, cloaked
in feathers?

*I spent four sleepless
lifetimes in another world.
You stand under these green hazels
like I don't know you,
stranger. But she asked me to meet you
here. Can you say
her name?*

You know I can't
sleep I can't
name her.
What did she want you
to sing?

*I was a long time waiting
for a word, through snow,
through dark winter. In the end
I left with the leaves.*

And what word
fell with you?
Winged leaf, is there nothing for me?

The going down of the sun

Michael came back from his war
without much noise, with a head
full of stories he'd never tell
and most of his life already lived,
though he was still in his twenties.
He supposed the Falklands
wasn't an important war,
and the tours in Ireland
always a tricky topic,
so he didn't expect to be asked
about his time and didn't mind
when he wasn't. He found it odd
no one went to any trouble
to re-integrate him. He found it hard
to think like a civvy.
His dreams were all explosions
and his marriage didn't last.
Around the time he lost
his job he also lost all access
to his son, and that
was when things started downhill.

You see him round Oxford
town centre now, having decided
too late that he did in fact mind
what happened to him, he had
in fact wanted that homecoming party.
Few listen long enough to learn

the problem. He has a way
of grabbing your hand to shake
then not letting go, getting violent
if you offer help, and repeating
in a ruined voice *Do you see
these tattoos? Did you know when I was young
I could have played for Chelsea?*

The Solitary Reader

What the fat boy
who went to the library lunchtimes
after handing out biscuits and milk
and keeping too much for himself
didn't get was the point of it all.
The books he read, the days
and nights he spent alone
with someone else's hardback, castoff love
never led him to anything
he could hold. It was only later,
years after the shell around him
hardened, that he saw
stories had no point in themselves.
The only use of a book
was to help you put the thing down,
walk away from the desk
and live.

And by tracing it twice

1. *Fritilleries*

   The heads hang like a photograph
   of rain in the moment before it darns
   the grass, and seem
   as soft as foxgloves did

   when we were children. If
   I touched them, put the tip
   of a finger in the cave where the bees drink,
   they would feel like wings.

   Look. The tip of the tongue
   of the past is waiting there
   to speak shell-like of the days
   we learned the names of flowers.

2. *Leaving Bruges*

Whenever we went into tunnels
our ears popped, except
on the way home when you slept.
Out the window the day unravelled

around us, straw loam and pasture,
tractors writing fields,
baths and old wheels
full of grain, drained of water.

Your feet were between mine
and you slept against the angled
window, hair tumbled
over your face. I watched the line

of the sky as the earth swelled
like a breast, tree-topped,
plump soil and rock
riddled with light. You slept well,

mouth half-open, your cheek
as soft as the hand
you put on my hand
when you stirred in St Pancras and woke.

3. *Blue Stone*

> I have been imagining the house
> that I will build for us
> from the raw material of my days;
>
> the roof I will put over our heads
> with my words, if I live
> well enough to earn the slate.
>
> The Welsh half of me
> is from slate country, and I know
> how it layers and works;
>
> how it locks up, wraps up
> fossils like secrets within itself.
> That will be us. We will build
>
> secret walls around ourselves,
> and be safe there, and happy and warm
> in the knowledge that we are secret.
>
> Don't worry; the house I will build for us
> will not be closed like slate.
> I will fill it with light, like you like it.

4. *The Violin*

When you are away,
I spend my time with a ghost you,
a thought of you
to whom I tell all the day's events.

But my thoughts
don't reach your real ears, and
only your ghost self
hears them - so the love I think

I am building on
is undeveloped. New things I tell
for you stay secret:
the words go, the unimportant thoughts

that make a life.
That is why I am carving you this
violin. It is
a solid thought that I can give.

I found this
torn strip of wood on the canal path
shortcut back from
seeing you off; it has started to look

like an owl
taking flight; a Georgia O'Keefe; a
malformed elephant;
a harp. When you are away, my love,

you haunt me;
so I am whittling the hours till you come home.
This won't sing, but
the love that made it did, my violinist.

5. *Morning*

   Saturday morning, eight o'clock;
   the light through the blinds
   finds us out, and we part,
   wake, then lie stirring,
   legs interwoven
   amid the hot sheets
   the heartbeats
   until our eyes peel open and we see
   each other's faces, you and me.